Dark Was the Night

WRITTEN BY
GARY GOLIO

ILLUSTRATED BY
E.B. LEWIS

 Nancy Paulsen Books

Even in the deep darkness of outer space,
   there is light...

1977

A science probe, strapped to a rocket, is shot into space.

Voyager I, bearing a precious Golden Record, a message
   to the Universe from Planet Earth.

With pictures—of people, children, snowflakes, and sky.

With sounds—of thunder, crickets, whales, and the wind.

With music—of Navajo chants, Peruvian panpipes, West
   African drumming, Beethoven, and even Chuck Berry.

And one ghostly song, about loneliness and the night.

A musician, playing his guitar and humming a tune of light
   and hope to whoever might be listening. A human being,
   reaching out to the stars.

A blind man named Willie Johnson.

1897

You were born in the light, Willie Johnson.

On a January day. In a small Texas town.

As a boy, you loved to sing. So your
father made a cigar box guitar,
and you learned to play.

But then your mama died, and some light
went out of your life.
At seven or eight you went blind, and that's
when things got darker still.

So how does a blind boy get along?
How does he make his way in the world?

Being blind didn't stop a person from
singing in church, or on street corners.
   Besides, this was a way to use your words,
and your voice, to lift people up.
   Now you were back in the light.

You used your singing voice the way a preacher would—
sometimes loud and rough, sometimes soft and tender.
After all, there was sadness in the world, but also joy.

You sang gospel songs like they were the blues, which
weren't allowed in church.

And you took the blade of a pocketknife, ran it along
the steel strings of your guitar, to play what was called *slide*.
This made a sound like someone laughing or crying, as if
the guitar had a voice of its own.

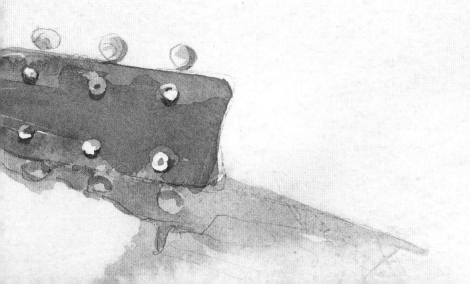

Now, Texas is a big place. So you traveled from one town
to another the easiest way a blind man could—by train.

Marlin, Temple, Hearne, Brenham, Beaumont.
That's how you saw the world.

On Saturdays, cotton farmers came into town to mingle and buy food. Out on the street, you'd stand tall in your jacket and tie, singing in a rough and tender voice as you slid your pocketknife along the strings.

Your raspy growling was soothed by sweet words
calling everyone to live a good life.

In return, people put coins in your tin cup so you
could eat and have a place to sleep that night.

Town to town, corner to corner, church to church—you kept getting better at what you did. People came to know your name.

Then a man from a music company heard you sing. You were given the chance to make a record, something people could buy and listen to on their home phonographs.

In a dark, quiet room, your voice poured into a microphone, slid down some wires, and scratched itself onto a wax disc. The record caught you breathing, singing, and moving your knife along those steel strings.

It was the sound of one human being reaching out to all the others, telling them not to be afraid of the dark.

After all, if a blind man could see the light . . .

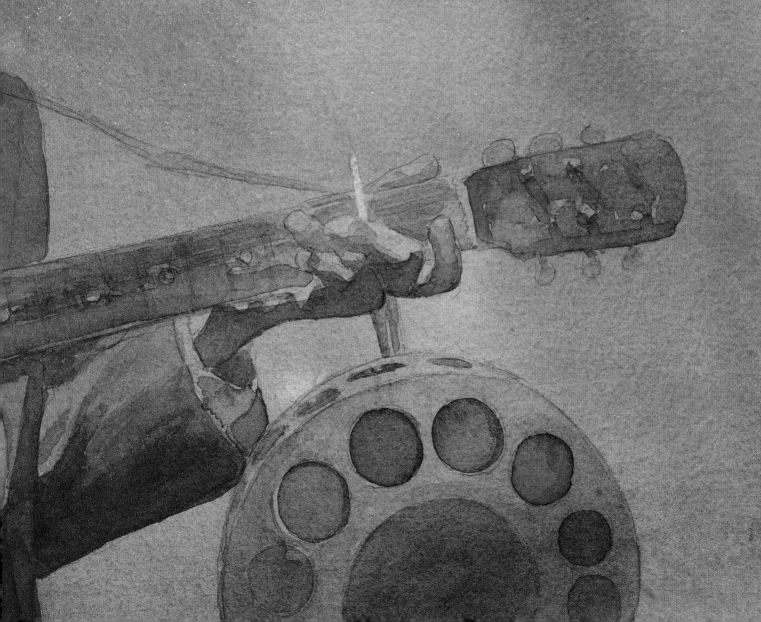

Your first record sold thousands of copies and was played on the radio.

Ads in the newspaper said of your singing and guitar playing that there was "Nothing like it anywhere else!"

One of your songs, "Dark Was the Night," is just you playing slide, humming and moaning. It was a ray of light that touched people deep in their souls.

Suddenly, you were a shining star.

With the sun glinting off your pocketknife, you kept spreading the light.

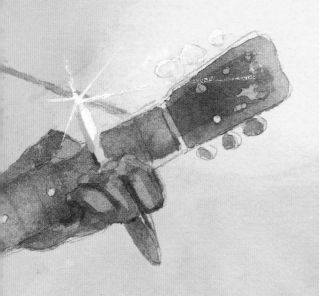

Time passed. Yet after you died, your
voice echoed down through the years.
It even found its way onto a golden disc,
sent into space, where it shined a light in
the darkness and finally touched the stars.

The Mystery of Blind Willie Johnson

Music lovers have known about Willie Johnson's music since his records first came out in 1928. What we *didn't* know much about was Willie himself. But since his death in 1945, writers, historians, and admirers of his work have been tirelessly researching his life. This has meant digging through birth and death records in town and county courthouses, looking through microfilm photographs of old newspapers, and talking to people who knew or were related to the man himself. Not surprisingly, with ongoing research like this, each new bit of information sparks still more questions, leading devoted music lovers in ever new directions. It's exciting to imagine what details of Willie's life will be discovered in the years to come!

For now, *Dark Was the Night* is based on the facts as we know them, but it's the simple beauty of Willie's playing and the magic he creates with his voice that are most important. His song "Dark Was the Night" reminds us that we're not alone—even in this immense universe—because we're tightly connected by what we all feel at one time or another: loneliness, love, sadness, and hope. So you should listen to Willie sing that song yourself by finding a recording of his music either in the library or online. It's haunting and unforgettable, and may even make you less afraid of the dark.

The Golden Record

In 1977, NASA made a time capsule of sorts, called the Golden Record, to send out into space aboard *Voyager I*. It was meant to portray the diversity of life on Earth and to promote peace. When scientist and astronomer Carl Sagan was choosing the sounds for the record, he asked renowned music historian Alan Lomax to help him. Lomax added songs and music from cultures all over the world, including Navajo Indian chants, jazz (Louis Armstrong), and rock and roll (Chuck Berry). His goal was to give the biggest picture of human-made sounds and the feelings they expressed. For that reason, Willie Johnson's wordless song "Dark Was the Night" was included right next to a string quartet by Beethoven. Lomax believed that Johnson powerfully conveyed the sense of loneliness that all people feel—something very important to know about human beings and life on planet Earth.

And who is the Golden Record meant for? The U.S. president at the time, Jimmy Carter, said this in his introduction:

We cast this message into the cosmos. . . . Of the 200 billion stars in the Milky Way galaxy, some—perhaps many—may have inhabited planets and spacefaring civilizations. If one such civilization intercepts Voyager *and can understand these recorded contents, here is our message:* **This is a present from a small distant world, a token of our sounds, our science, our images, our music, our thoughts, and our feelings. . . .** *This record represents our hope and our determination and our good will in a vast and awesome universe.*

On August 25, 2012, *Voyager I*—traveling through space at 38,000 miles per hour—became the first human-made object to leave our solar system and journey so far from Earth. On it is the song of a blind man, someone who knew both light and darkness, bearing a message of hope to the stars themselves.

For my friend E. B. Lewis, who conjures darkness and light.
—G. G.

Dedicated to the congregation of
Corinthian Baptist Church, of North Philadelphia,
for their participation and support.
—E. B. L.

Sources and Resources

Blakey, D. N. *Revelation: Blind Willie Johnson: The Biography*. DNB45 Publishing, 2007.

Corcoran, Michael. "The Soul of Blind Willie Johnson." *Austin American Statesman*, September 28, 2003.

Ford, Shane. *Shine a Light: My Year with "Blind" Willie Johnson*. Lulu.com, 2011.

Hall, Michael. "The Soul of a Man: Who Was Blind Willie Johnson?" *Texas Monthly*, December 2010.

Johnson, Willie. *Dark Was the Night*. Columbia/Legacy, 1998.

Visit *Voyager—The Golden Record*, part of NASA's Jet Propulsion Laboratory website, for video, images, history, and news. The *Voyager*'s photos of our solar system and planets are breathtaking, and kids will especially enjoy the Scenes of Earth, found on the Golden Record.

voyager.jpl.nasa.gov/golden-record/

NANCY PAULSEN BOOKS
An imprint of Penguin Random House LLC, New York

Nancy Paulsen Books is a trademark of Penguin Random House LLC.

Visit us online at penguinrandomhouse.com

Library of Congress Cataloging-in-Publication Data is available.

Manufactured in China by RR Donnelley Asia Printing Solutions Ltd.
ISBN 9781524738884
10 9 8 7 6 5 4 3 2 1

Design by Suki Boynton • Text set in LTC Cloister Pro • The art was done in watercolor.